Muhammad Ali

A Little Golden Book® Biography

T0354259

By Frank Berrios · Illustrated by Ken Daley

A GOLDEN BOOK • NEW YORK

Text copyright © 2024 by Frank Berrios
Cover art and interior illustrations copyright © 2024 by Ken Daley
All rights reserved. Published in the United States by Golden Books, an imprint of Random
House Children's Books, a division of Penguin Random House LLC, 1745 Broadway,
New York, NY 10019. Golden Books, A Golden Book, A Little Golden Book, the G colophon,
and the distinctive gold spine are registered trademarks of Penguin Random House LLC.
rhcbooks.com
Educators and librarians, for a variety of teaching tools, visit us at RHTeachersLibrarians.com
Library of Congress Control Number: 2023930092
ISBN 978-0-593-70389-2 (trade) — ISBN 978-0-593-70390-8 (ebook)
Printed in the United States of America
10 9 8 7 6 5 4 3 2 1

Muhammad Ali was born Cassius Marcellus Clay Jr. in Louisville, Kentucky, on January 17, 1942. His father, Cassius Marcellus Clay Sr., painted murals and billboard signs for local stores and businesses. His mother, Odessa Clay, worked as a cook and a maid. Younger brother Rudy completed the family.

Louisville, Kentucky, was segregated in the 1940s. White and Black people couldn't live in the same neighborhoods, go to the same schools, or shop in the same stores, and Black people were only allowed to sit in the back of the bus. From a very young age, Cassius knew that he wasn't welcome everywhere he went.

Nevertheless, Cassius and Rudy had a happy childhood. Their parents worked hard to provide them with a loving home and family.

When Cassius was twelve years old, he and a friend rode their bikes into town.

When it was time to head home, Cassius discovered his bike had been stolen!

Cassius was heartbroken—he loved his bicycle!
A passerby told him to report the theft to a police
officer who was coaching young boxers in a nearby
gym. Cassius told the officer, Joe Martin, that he
wanted to find the person who stole his bike. Officer
Martin offered to teach Cassius how to box just in
case he found the thief.

Before long, Cassius was a regular at Columbia Gym. When the gym was closed, he worked out at a nearby community center with another trainer named Fred Stoner. Both trainers helped Cassius develop his speed and style in the ring.

At first, Cassius wasn't a good boxer—but he *was* a hard worker. He was also very confident and often bragged about how one day he would be the best fighter in the world!

All of Cassius's hard work paid off. By age sixteen, he had won six Kentucky Golden Gloves and two national Golden Gloves titles!

Cassius next began training for the 1960 Olympics in Rome, Italy. The young boxer easily made the Olympic team.

In Rome, Cassius was friendly with athletes from all around the globe. He was so popular he became known as the mayor of the Olympic Village, the place where athletes live during the Games.

Cassius used his fast feet and hands to beat talented boxers from Belgium, Russia, Australia, and Poland. He won the Olympic gold medal in boxing!

When the Olympics were over, Cassius flew back to his hometown of Louisville, Kentucky. Crowds of people came to cheer for the Olympic champion and give him a hero's welcome.

Cassius met a famous wrestler named Gorgeous George, who would taunt and tease his opponents and fans. Cassius liked his style. He thought it was a great way to attract an audience and sell tickets.

Cassius began to boast about how pretty, fast, and strong he was. His fans loved it! Before long, his fights were sold out.

By 1963, Cassius was the top contender for the heavyweight title. Charles "Sonny" Liston was the current heavyweight champion. Cassius would have to beat him to become the new champ.

"I am the greatest!"

"Float like a butterfly! Sting like a bee!" bragged Cassius, talking about his fast feet and powerful punches.

Sonny Liston was a tough fighter. No one thought Cassius would win. Incredibly, he beat Liston in just six rounds. Twenty-two-year-old Cassius was now the heavyweight champion of the world! He would even defeat Liston again a year later.

Soon after the first Liston fight, Cassius announced that he had become a Muslim and joined the Nation of Islam. Malcolm X, who spoke out against racism and inequality in America, was a well-known member of the Nation of Islam. The two men became friends.

Cassius began to speak out against racism, too. As a sign of his growing faith, he even changed his name to Muhammad Ali.

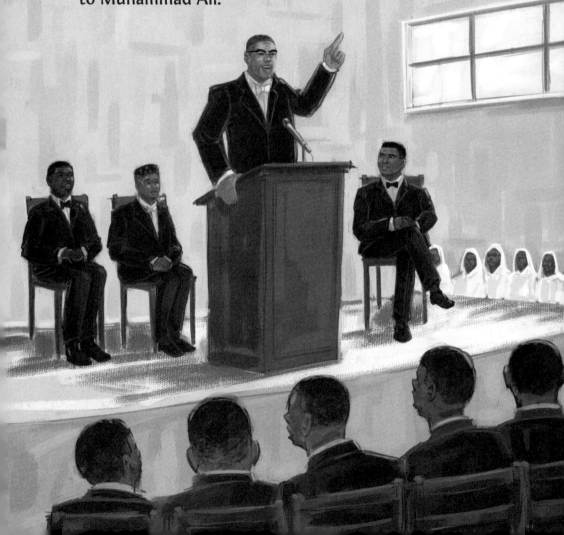

In the 1960s, the United States was involved in a war in Vietnam. Due to his religious beliefs, Ali was against the war. He refused to join the army when he was drafted in 1967.

Ali knew he could go to jail for not going to war. He could even lose his championship title. But Ali followed his heart and did what he thought was right.

Ali's championship title and boxing license were taken away, but he continued to speak out. He gave anti-war lectures at colleges and universities around the country. More and more people began to agree with him that the war in Vietnam was wrong.

Ali went to court to win back his boxing license, and after three long years, he won. Sports fans were thrilled when Ali returned to the ring in 1970!

Ali would face some of his fiercest opponents during the 1970s. He suffered his first professional loss at the hands of Joe Frazier in 1971. George Foreman would go on to beat Frazier in 1973.

The next year in Zaire, a country on the continent of Africa, Ali snatched back the championship title from George Foreman in a fight called the "Rumble in the Jungle."

Ali eventually lost the championship to Leon Spinks in 1978. But the young boxer wasn't champ for long. Ali came back that same year and beat Spinks, winning the championship for a third time—a first in boxing history!

But his biggest battle was yet to come. In 1984, Ali was diagnosed with Parkinson's, a disease that affects a person's ability to control their muscles and movements. Ali was fearless in his fight to raise awareness and money in search of a cure for the disease.

In 1996, Muhammad Ali was asked to play a big part in the opening ceremony for the Summer Olympics in Atlanta, Georgia. He accepted the request and proudly lit the Olympic flame as three billion people around the world watched.

Muhammad Ali passed away on June 3, 2016. He was an amazing athlete and activist who overcame incredible odds to become the heavyweight champion of the world. His actions, both inside and outside the ring, continue to inspire people today. That's why Muhammad Ali will forever be known as the Greatest of All Time!